EXPLORING OUR OCEANS

ANGLERFISH

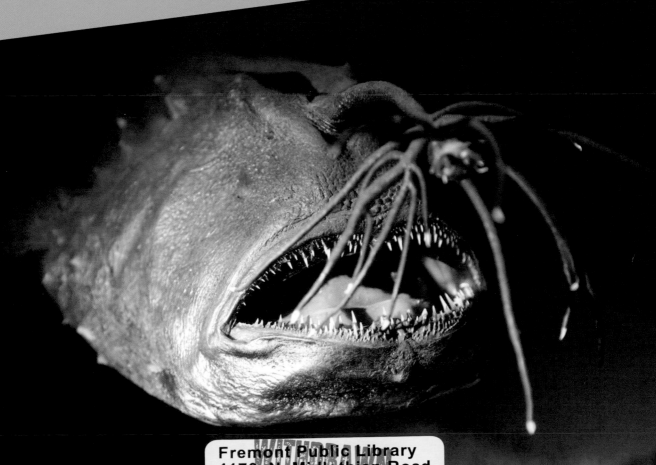

JULIE MURPHY

Published in the United States of America by Cherry Lake Publishing
Ann Arbor, Michigan
www.cherrylakepublishing.com

Consultants: Dominique A. Didier, PhD, Associate Professor, Department of Biology, Millersville University;
Marla Conn, ReadAbility, Inc.
Book design: Sleeping Bear Press

Photo Credits: ©Kasparart/Dreamstime.com, cover, 1, 15; ©MikaelEriksson/Thinkstock, 5; ©New Zealand-American
Submarine Ring of Fire 2005 Exploration; NOAA Vents Program/http://www.flickr.com/CC-BY-2.0, 6; ©Susana_Mar-
tins/Shutterstock Images, 7; ©NOAA/NMFS/SEFSC Pascagoula Laboratory; Collection of Brandi Noble, NOAA/NMFS/
SEFSC/http://www.flickr.com/CC-BY-2.0, 8; ©NOAA Okeanos Explorer Program, INDEX-SATAL 2010, NOAA/OER/
http://www.flickr.com/CC-BY-2.0, 11; ©Dorling Kindersley/Thinkstock, 12; ©NOAA Ocean Explorer/http://www.flickr.
com/CC-BY-SA 2.0, 13; ©bierchen/Shutterstock Images, 17; ©Ethan Daniels/Shutterstock Images, 18; ©Ye Choh Wah/
Shutterstock Images, 19; ©Silke Baron/Shutterstock Images, 21; ©Silke Baron/http://www.flickr.com/CC-BY-2.0, 23;
©Sally Reader/Australian Museum, 24; ©Helena moedermens/http://www.flickr.com/CC-BY-2.0, 27; ©Richard
Whitcombe/Shutterstock Images, 28

Library of Congress Cataloging-in-Publication Data

Murphy, Julie, 1965- author.
Anglerfish / by Julie Murphy.
        pages cm. — (Exploring our oceans)
  Summary: "Discover facts about anglerfish, including physical features, habitat, life cycle, food,
and threats to these ocean creatures. Photos, captions, and keywords supplement the narrative of
this informational text"—Provided by publisher.
  Audience: Age 8-12.
  Audience: Grades 4 to 6.
  Includes bibliographical references and index.
  ISBN 978-1-63188-024-7 (hardcover)—ISBN 978-1-63188-067-4 (pbk.)— ISBN 978-1-63188-110-7 (pdf)—
ISBN 978-1-63188-153-4 (ebook) 1. Anglerfishes—Juvenile literature. I. Title. II. Title: Anglerfish.
III. Series: 21st century skills library. Exploring our oceans.

QL637.9.L6M87 2015
597.62—dc23   2014005276

Cherry Lake Publishing would like to acknowledge the work of
The Partnership for 21st Century Skills. Please visit www.p21.org
for more information.

Printed in the United States of America
Corporate Graphics Inc.

ABOUT THE AUTHOR

Julie Murphy is an Australian children's writer. She trained in zoology and zookeeping and loves
writing about animals. She also enjoys traveling. Julie lives in Melbourne with her husband and
daughter and their pets.

TABLE OF CONTENTS

Fish That Go Fishing

The anglerfish is a very strange-looking sea creature. Just look at its huge mouth, sharp teeth, and round, blobby body. It even has a weird spine shaped like a fishing rod sticking out of its head! No wonder this fish lurks in the lonely, dark depths of the sea. If you looked like this, wouldn't you?

Anglerfish is actually a term that describes a group of more than 300 **species** of fish. Scientists call this group the Lophiiformes. Different species in this group

[21ST CENTURY SKILLS LIBRARY]

also go by common names such as goosefish, monkfish, sea devil, sea toad, coffinfish, frogmouth, frogfish, and batfish.

This monkfish has a bumpy body that helps it blend in with its surroundings.

Anglerfish live in every ocean and major sea of the world. They are found in a wide range of **habitats**, including deep oceans, coastlines, and coral reefs. Some live in the open water. Others live on the sea bottom. One very strange anglerfish from Australia even makes its home where rivers meet the sea. It lives in a mix of salty and fresh water, less than 3 feet (1 m) deep!

This anglerfish seems to almost have legs.

This frogfish glides along the ocean floor.

The anglerfish has a special spine called an illicium.

illicium

LOOK AGAIN

LOOK CLOSELY AT THE ANGLERFISH IN THIS PHOTOGRAPH.
WHAT CAN YOU LEARN ABOUT THE ILLICIUM
THAT YOU HAVEN'T LEARNED FROM THIS CHAPTER?

Anglerfish get their name from the word *angler*. An angler is a person who catches fish using a rod, line, and bait. The anglerfish's fishing rod is called an **illicium**. This modified spine looks a lot like an angler's fishing rod. And it works like one, too! Anglerfish are **carnivores**. They use their illicium to catch fish to eat. That's right—they are fish that go fishing! ◂

Spongy Balls and Pancakes

Like all animals, anglerfish are suited to their habitat. And they don't all look the same. Deep-sea species can look like spongy versions of the ball used to play dodgeball. Ones from shallower waters look like pointy-toothed pancakes!

Viewed from the front, the flattened body of the goosefish looks a lot like a pancake. This anglerfish lives at the bottom of shallow seas, near coastlines. It has a huge mouth and rows of small, sharp teeth. The mouth

[21ST CENTURY SKILLS LIBRARY]

and two large eyes point upward. The illicium points up from between the goosefish's eyes. It has a fleshy **lure** called an **esca** on its tip.

Anglerfish can come in many shapes and sizes. Which other animals does this one remind you of?

BODY DIAGRAM

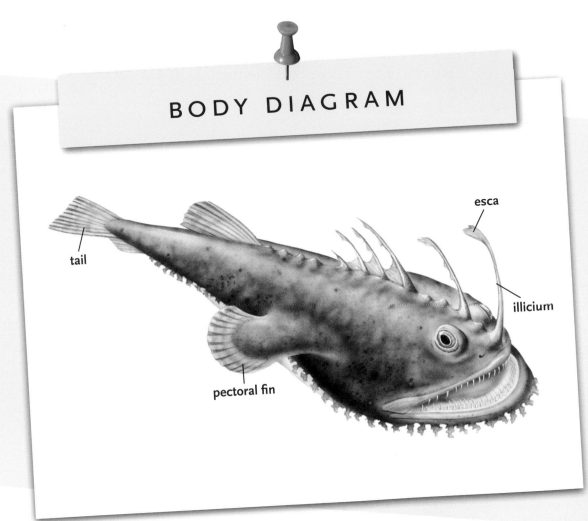

esca

tail

illicium

pectoral fin

Anglerfish are different sizes, colors, and shapes.

This anglerfish uses its fins as feet to help it climb up rocks.

The goosefish does its best to blend in with its habitat. Its skin is dark and bumpy, and has no scales. There is a fleshy border around the body that looks like seaweed. This great disguise helps the goosefish to avoid predators and catch food. Most anglerfishes are relatively small, with females being much larger than males. Goosefish are an exception. The largest recorded goosefish was nearly 6.5 feet (2 m) long and weighed almost 132 pounds (60 kg).

Batfishes have fins that work like little feet. Yes, this strange fish actually walks along the sea bottom! They have a single **dorsal** fin along the back. The body ends in a tail.

The black sea devil looks quite different from its coastal cousin, the goosefish. That's because it lives about 10,000 feet (3,048 m) underwater. The sea devil's body is built to cope with the pressure of the deep sea. Its body is small, round, and spongy, and can withstand the water's weight. It is roughly the same shape and size as a ball used to play dodgeball.

The sea devil is dark colored. This helps it to blend in with the darkness all around it. It has small eyes and a huge mouth with long, curved, needle-sharp fangs. Its illicium has a globe-shaped lure, the esca, on the end. And, like a real globe, it gives off light! The light is actually made by millions of tiny **bacteria** that live within the esca.

GO DEEPER

FIND ANOTHER SOURCE OF INFORMATION ABOUT SEA CREATURES THAT HAVE GLOWING QUALITIES. CAN YOU FIND THE TERM FOR A CREATURE'S ABILITY TO GIVE OFF LIGHT?

The dark skin of this black sea devil helps it blend into the deepest part of the ocean.

Eating Anything!

Anglerfish are predators. But unlike many predators, they catch prey by being sneaky instead of being fast. The anglerfish sits very still and is **camouflaged**. Then it goes fishing. It slowly moves its illicium around. The lure on the tip of the illicium acts as bait. The lure's job is to attract the interest of any nearby animals. In anglerfish that live in shallow water, the lure wriggles. This makes it look like a little swimming animal. In many deep-sea anglerfish, the lure glows with a soft light, which is easily seen in the darkness.

Anglerfish don't need to move quickly to catch their prey.

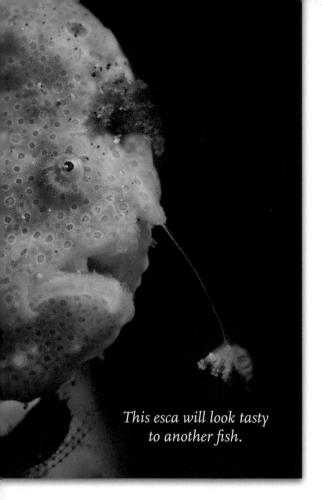

This esca will look tasty to another fish.

When a curious fish comes closer, the anglerfish holds the lure directly in front of its own mouth. The prey comes even closer. Just before the prey bites the tasty-looking lure, the anglerfish opens its mouth. Water rushes into the big, gaping hole and sucks the victim in along with it. The fish is eaten whole.

Anglerfish make the most of every chance they get to eat. Thanks to stretchy jaws and stomachs, anglerfish are able to eat very large prey. Some anglerfish can eat prey twice their own size. That would be a bit like you eating a sheep in one gulp! Shallow-water anglerfish eat crustaceans, small fish, and even each other! The goosefish can eat just about anything it wants including small sharks, fish and even some seabirds.

This hairy frogfish might look like a harmless plant to other animals.

A strange specimen at the Natural History Museum in London, England, had puzzled staff for more than 10 years. The specimen was a deep-sea hairy anglerfish. The puzzle was its huge stomach. Why was the stomach so big? The specimen was rare, so scientists didn't want to damage it by cutting open the stomach to look inside.

A special machine called a CT scanner solved the riddle. The machine took thousands of x-rays of the anglerfish. This allowed the museum staff to build a 3-D model of the fish inside and out. What was in the stomach? A fish, all in knots. When stretched out, the fish was twice as long as the predator that ate it!

This giant frogfish blends in with the coral.

LOOK AGAIN

Look closely at this photograph. What do you notice about an anglerfish's body that allows it to be such a successful predator?

TOGETHER FOREVER

In some anglerfish species, the male uses his eyes and nostrils to look for and sniff out a mate. Some scientists wonder if deep-sea females help out by using their glowing lures as a sign to say, "I'm over here!" In some species, the males cannot see or smell very well. And their females lack glowing lures. How these fish manage to pair up remains a mystery.

Some species of deep-sea anglerfish have a very unusual mating strategy. Once a male and female anglerfish do manage to meet, the male bites into his

[21ST CENTURY SKILLS LIBRARY]

mate with sharp little teeth. And he doesn't let go. Over time, the male's and female's skin joins. Their blood mixes together. The male becomes part of the female's body!

This anglerfish is not fully grown.

A male gets all the energy he needs from the food his mate has eaten. Bits of the male's body that are no longer needed are gradually lost. But he keeps his **testes**. The

The anglerfish has a complicated way of reproducing.

LOOK AGAIN

Look closely at this photograph. After reading about how some anglerfish breed, what do you think is happening here?

[21ST CENTURY SKILLS LIBRARY]

testes make **sperm**, which will **fertilize** the female's eggs to make baby anglerfish. Once joined, the male provides a never-ending supply of sperm. Some females have six or more males attached!

The female anglerfish releases eggs from her body, and the male releases sperm from his. The eggs and sperm join together in the seawater to form new lives.

Goosefish have a different strategy. A female goosefish releases up to a million eggs at a time. The eggs are protected in a long ribbon of jelly called an egg raft. Goosefish are the only fish known to make egg rafts. Inside the egg raft, each egg has its own private room with flow-through "air-conditioning" to keep the egg healthy.

When the larvae hatch out of the egg raft, they look like tiny adults. Young goosefish males take about four years to grow up. Females take about five years. They can live for up to 20 years.

THREATS

No predators depend on anglerfish for their food. However, some large animals will eat anglerfish if they get the chance. These predators include the conger eel, Atlantic cod, bigger anglerfish, and whales. But even without major predators, anglerfish face a number of threats. Sadly, most of them are from people.

People catch anglerfish for food as well as for pets. The goosefish is commercially fished and sold as monkfish in North America. Anglerfish also make interesting and unusual additions to the family fish tank.

What would you do if you saw this on your dinner plate?

This green frogfish is hiding, but is still in danger of predators.

Sometimes fishing **trawlers** catch deep-sea anglerfish by accident. These fish always die because their bodies cannot survive near the water's surface. They are suited to life far beneath the surface.

Pollution and climate change also threaten anglerfish. Waste can be washed by rainwater through drainpipes into the sea where fish live. Climate change threatens the entire world's wildlife, including anglerfish. It affects the world's weather patterns and sea temperatures. Air pollution is making climate change happen faster than normal.

The good side to knowing very little about some anglerfish is that there are still exciting discoveries to make. In 2013, for example, four new anglerfish species were discovered near New Zealand. They were all deep-sea fish with glow-in-the-dark lures. Awesome!

Anglerfish have lived on Earth for around 160 million years. Let's do our best to make sure they stick around for a lot longer.

THINK ABOUT IT
DO YOU THINK THERE SHOULD BE LAWS TO PREVENT PEOPLE FROM FISHING FOR ANGLERFISH? WHAT IF SOME COMMUNITIES DEPEND ON ANGLERFISH FOR FOOD?

THINK ABOUT IT

- What was the most surprising fact you learned from reading this book?

- In chapter 5, we learned that people eat anglerfish. Would you like to taste anglerfish? Why? What might happen if people caught so many anglerfish that some species became extinct?

- Go online or visit the library to find more information about anglerfish. Compare the information you find there with the information in this book.

LEARN MORE

FURTHER READING

Lunis, Natalie. *Glow-in-the-Dark Animals*. New York: Bearport, 2011.

Lynette, Rachel. *Deep-Sea Anglerfish and Other Fearsome Fish*. Chicago: Raintree, 2012.

Niver, Heather Moore. *20 Fun Facts About Anglerfish*. New York: Gareth Stevens, 2013.

WEB SITES

Animal Planet—Anglerfish
http://animal.discovery.com/fish/anglerfish-info.htm
Learn more interesting facts about many different anglerfish.

ARKive—Anglerfish
www.arkive.org/anglerfish/lophius-piscatorius/video-08.html
Watch a video of an anglerfish catching a smaller fish.

National Geographic—Anglerfish
http://animals.nationalgeographic.com/animals/fish/anglerfish
Read more about anglerfish and look at a map of where this strange creature lives.

GLOSSARY

bacteria (bak-TEER-ee-uh) single cell organisms so small you need a microscope to see them

camouflaged (KAM-uh-flahjd) when an animal's natural coloring enables it to blend in with its surroundings

carnivores (KAHR-nuh-vorz) animals that eat other animals

cold-blooded (KOHLD BLUHD-id) having a body temperature that changes according to the temperature of the surroundings

dorsal (DORL-suhl) on or toward the back of an animal

esca (ESS-kah) fleshy tip, or lure, at the tip of an anglerfishes illicium

fertilize (FUR-tuh-lyz) to cause an egg to develop into a new organism by adding male reproductive material

habitats (HAB-ih-tats) the places where animals or plants naturally live

illicium (il-IS-ee-um) modified dorsal spine that forms the fishing rod of the anglerfish

lure (LOOR) something that has a strong power to attract

species (SPEE-sheez) one type, or kind, of plant or animal

sperm (SPURM) male reproductive cell

testes (TES-teez) male reproductive organs that produce sperm

trawlers (TRAW-lerz) fishing boats that drag a net to catch fish

INDEX